Jackie Robinson: The Inspiring Story of One of Baseball's Greatest Legends

An Unauthorized Biography

By: Clayton Geoffreys

Table of Contents

Foreword

Jackie Robinson fundamentally changed the game of baseball, by ushering in a new era that allowed for players of all colors to play the game they love in the modern era. Robinson was a quintessential superstar who carried himself the right way on and off the field. His use of nonviolence in a turbulent time for American society set an example for others, as he blazed the path for the end of racial segregation in professional baseball. Following his death, Jackie Robinson was awarded the Congressional Gold Medal and Presidential Medal of Freedom for his legacy on and off the field. Thank you for purchasing *Jackie Robinson: The Inspiring Story of One of Baseball's Greatest Legends*. In this unauthorized biography, we will learn Jackie Robinson's incredible life story and impact on the game of baseball. Hope you enjoy and if you do, please do not forget to leave a review!

Also, check out my website at claytongeoffreys.com to join my exclusive list where I let you know about my latest books. To thank you for your purchase, you can go to my site to download a free copy of *33 Life Lessons: Success Principles, Career Advice & Habits of Successful People*. In the book, you'll learn from some of the greatest thought leaders of different industries on what it takes to become successful and how to live a great life.

Cheers,

Clayton Geoffreys

Visit me at www.claytongeoffreys.com

Introduction

"Whether our forebears were strangers who crossed the Atlantic or the Pacific or the Rio Grande, we are here only because this country welcomed them in and taught them that to be an American is about something more than what we look like, or what our last names are, or how we worship." – Barack Obama, 44th president of the United States.

What Obama said in that statement carries a huge weight in the world of professional sports today. We are now seeing different races of people who have come from all sorts of countries, regardless of their color and their religion, performing well in the grandest stage, as America has allowed them to flourish and hone their talents to become the best they could ever be. Sports has become an area where race no longer matters and where we see people of any color or creed coming out on top to fight against the odds.

Of course, things were not always that way. In the past, not a lot of people of color were able to succeed in sports because they did not have the same opportunities as the Caucasian athletes of yesteryear. In basketball, it took until the 1950 season for Earl Lloyd to become the first African American player to be drafted into the NBA. Meanwhile, NBA legend Bill Russell spent his entire career fighting for civil rights for the African American people. In the NFL, Kenny Washington became the first African American player to sign with a professional football team in the modern era of the league but was signed only when the Los Angeles Rams went under fire amidst the league's ban against interracial players.

All such players contributed greatly to the rise of African Americans and other mixed-race players in their respective leagues. Even at this moment, African Americans dominate the NBA and the NFL landscape, as the majority of their best players are actually black. Had it not been for their forebears who helped pave the way for them to make it to their respective leagues, it might have taken a while for African Americans to see the success they are now seeing in the major American professional sports leagues.

In baseball, it is no secret that the MLB has a dark past from back in the early 20th century when they practiced what is known as the *color line*. Back when the modern version of the MLB began, teams had an unspoken "gentlemen's agreement" that essentially prevented them from signing people of color—or more specifically, African Americans, as light-skinned Hispanic Americans were actually allowed to play in the league. This was far from what the MLB was during the 19th century when they were allowing African Americans to play in the league. But, during the early portion of the 20th century, team owners were keen on taking segregation all the way to the MLB, as they simply did not want African Americans entering the league. Although there were no written rules supporting this policy, African Americans were nonetheless forced to play in what was called the Negro League back in the day.[i]

Come the 1940s, integration champion Branch Rickey started laying the foundation for bringing in the modern MLB's first black player when he joined the Brooklyn Dodgers. But, Rickey did not want to bring in just any player to cross the color line because he knew that he would be putting that player at risk and subjecting him to intense public scrutiny from people who did not exactly believe that line should be crossed. As such, Rickey vehemently believed that whoever he brought in from the Negro League should be someone good enough an athlete to give people a reason to believe that he should be in the MLB. The first player to break the color line also needed to be someone who had the mental fortitude that would allow him to block out all the insults he would be getting from those who did not agree with racial integration. Rickey thought that the man should be Jack Roosevelt Robinson, known as "Jackie" Robinson.

Jackie Robinson was always a natural athlete and was dominant in four different sports back when he played for UCLA. He later spent his pre-MLB days as a man who fought for the civil rights of his fellow black Americans. It started when he was drafted into the Army in 1942 during World War II. As a second lieutenant, he worked his way into establishing an officer candidate school solely for African Americans with the help of legendary boxer Joe Louis. While serving in the Army, he was even court-martialed for disobeying an order to move to the back of a bus.[i]

Jackie Robinson left the Army in 1944 and went on to play for the Negro League as a member of the Kansas City Monarchs. A year later, he met Branch Rickey, who was interested in what Robinson could do as a baseball player. He signed Jackie into a minor league contract with the Dodgers in preparation to eventually carry him into the MLB.

In 1947, Jackie Robinson officially crossed the MLB's long-standing color line by signing with the Brooklyn Dodgers to become the modern-day MLB's first-ever African American player. At 28 years old, he became the first African American to play in the MLB since 1884. He did so in front of a capacity crowd that consisted of at least 14,000 black Americans. Robinson's rise as an MLB player drew the attention of many black Americans all over the country as they went on to watch the Dodgers whenever playing different teams across America.

While there were positive responses to the Dodger's signing of Robinson, mutiny was brewing in the team's locker room, as there were white American players who said that they were not willing to play alongside a black player. A champion of Robinson's signing and a believer of what Jackie could do as a player, the team's manager, Leo Durocher, went on to say that he did not care about Jackie Robinson's color so long as he could play and could make the entire team successful. He basically shut the mutiny down by taking Robinson's side and making it clear that he was going to trade anyone who did not agree with the Brooklyn Dodgers' policy and belief in what Jackie Robinson could do as a player.

While Jackie Robinson could not completely avoid getting insulted and ridiculed by fellow players and baseball fans alike, he focused more on what he could do out there as a player. He received words of encouragement from fellow players and went on to earn friends and supporters of his own. Game respects game, as a lot of the best players in the MLB went on to support Jackie Robinson despite the odds being against the rising African American trailblazer.

The support he got from his peers and his strong will and determination to silence critics allowed Jackie Robinson to prove that he belonged in the MLB. He let his game do the talking for him and went on to win Major League Baseball's inaugural Rookie of the Year

Award and even went on to finish the season fifth in the MVP voting. Two years later, he went on to win the National League MVP to become the first African American player to win the award in the league's modern version.

Jackie Robinson continued to rise in skill and popularity. He was a six-time All-Star in the 10 years he spent in the MLB. He also played in the World Series six times and went on to win a championship in 1955. Based on what he was showing out there on the field, there was no arguing the fact that Robinson belonged in the MLB. And because of how talented he was, Robinson basically changed the way people saw segregation.

Even though he only spent 10 years in the MLB, Jackie Robinson spent much of his post-retirement days championing the Civil Rights Movement in a pacifist kind of way. Instead of advocating violence, he fought for his fellow black Americans by challenging traditional beliefs of what they should be. He succeeded as a businessman as well as a philanthropist.

Jackie Robinson did not get to live long enough to see his fellow African Americans dominating the world of sports and succeeding in the other fields of life as well. In 1972, he died of a heart attack. But, even after his death, he continued to change the way America perceived black Americans. He was posthumously awarded the Congressional Gold Medal and the Presidential Medal of Freedom for his influence in the Civil Rights Movement as a player, entrepreneur, and philanthropist.

It was in 1997 when the MLB gave him an honor no other player before him had ever earned. His jersey number 42 was retired across all MLB teams as he became the first-ever player in any professional league to be given such an honor. The league also announced in 2004 that April 15th was going to be called Jackie

Robinson Day, wherein all of the players in the MLB would wear his number 42 in recognition of what he had done for the sport and for America.

Jackie Robinson is not only one of the greatest athletes in the history of all the professional leagues across America, but also one of the most well-celebrated Americans in the 20th century. His life story is something that should be told over and over again because of what he has done and contributed to the sport of baseball and the Civil Rights Movement.

Chapter 1: Childhood and Early Life

Jack Roosevelt Robinson was born on January 31, 1919, in Cairo, Georgia, a small agricultural city with a population of only about 9,600 people in the most recent census. Given that Jackie was born into an agricultural community, the Robinsons were sharecroppers, which are farmers who are allowed by a landowner to use a portion of agricultural land in exchange for a share of the crops and the profits earned by the tenants while using the land. He was the youngest child out of five siblings born to parents Jerry and Mallie Robinson.

It is of no question that Jackie Robinson got his Roosevelt middle name from Theodore Roosevelt, the 26th president of the United States, who died just a few days before the youngest Robinson was born. Jackie's mother, Mallie, specifically chose Teddy Roosevelt's name for her son because he was one of the few leaders at that time who had a deep hatred for racism. It was Roosevelt who inspired many African Americans to rise up and speak against racism at a time when the United States was still decades away from granting equal civil rights to black Americans.[ii]

Roosevelt was famously known for speaking against white supremacy while also granting black Americans high offices in public service under his tenure and leadership as president. And though he was unsuccessful in the endeavor, Teddy Roosevelt tried his best to form a political coalition composed of black and white Americans. That being considered, it certainly was not a coincidence that Jackie Robinson eventually ended up as one of the more iconic black American figures—not only in baseball and in professional sports, but the entire history of the United States.

Growing up in Cairo, Georgia was not easy for Jackie Robinson or his family. The reason why Cairo was sometimes called "the land of the pharaohs" and "the

Egypt of the West" was not only because it was named after a place in the actual country of Egypt but also because slavery, to some extent, was practiced there by the pharaohs. However, the type of slavery practiced in the American town of Cairo and several nearby places in Georgia was more or less the practice of white Americans exploiting the need of African Americans to make a living for themselves. Sharecropping was seemingly one of those forms of slavery that the Robinsons had to endure at that time just to survive.

Even though Jerry and Mallie had the means to keep things afloat for their five children, things never really worked out for the family. Aside from the fact that Jerry and Mallie's marriage was never really perfect, the Robinsons had to endure a meager living and were forced to suffer under impoverished conditions in Georgia, which is not exactly known for being friendly towards black Americans. Moreover, relations between the blacks and the whites in that region were getting worse, as many African Americans were tired of the subpar conditions they were forced to live under. Riots began to occur, and the outlook was increasingly bleak for the Robinsons in Cairo. This prompted a need for a change of scenery for the infant Jackie and his family.

It was some time in 1920 when a friend on Mallie's side of the family helped the Robinsons escape from the harsh conditions in Georgia. Without Jerry, who had left the family earlier that same year, Mallie and her children proceeded to move west after her close family friend told her that opportunities and treatment of black Americans were a lot better there.[ii] The Robinsons moved to Pasadena, California and established a settlement there, where Mallie was forced to work all sorts of jobs just to try to make a living for the family.

While things were better in California than they were back in Georgia, blacks were still not treated with the same type of equality as the Robinsons expected when they moved there. Mallie did not have the luxury of choosing jobs because not a lot of employers were willing to take her on. That sparsity of available work forced her to do all sorts of jobs that were not exactly normal but still enabled her to feed her family.

Meanwhile, Jackie grew up without being able to enjoy the same kind of life that most California kids experienced. Pasadena may have been a "gold" neighborhood, but the Robinsons felt left out because they were poor. And on top of the fact that he did not have a true father figure to help him navigate through his childhood, Jackie was also excluded from the recreational activities that white kids were allowed to join back in that day.

Feeling lost and wanting to feel like he belonged, Jackie Robinson opted to join a street gang composed of black kids who similarly could not enjoy the same kind of lifestyle that white children had at that time. Luckily for Jackie, he had a voice of reason that helped him decide to soon abandon that kind of life. His friend, Carl Anderson, convinced him that joining a gang is not exactly the way he should live his life. As such, Jackie left life on the streets and allowed himself to focus on the more meaningful things in life.[iii] Had Jackie not decided to leave the neighborhood gang, things would have certainly turned out differently for the man who is now known as one of the greatest figures in all of American history.

Jackie Robinson had to focus his energy on something more concrete and meaningful than being part of a gang that simply could not steer him in the right direction. This focus was what allowed him to use his natural giftedness as an athlete to excel in all of the sports he played. Of course, it also helped that he had people to look up to. The Robinson siblings were composed of four males and one female: Jackie, Edgar, Frank, Matthew (aka "Mack"), and Willa Mae. Jackie idolized his older brothers, who were all great athletes in their own right. In fact, his brother Matthew (Mack) won a silver medal in the 1936 Olympics. He, along with his brother Frank, helped convince Jackie to pursue the life of an athlete at a time when there were not a lot of career options for African American youngsters. Inspired by his brothers, Jackie Robinson went on to focus on becoming a standout athlete.

Chapter 2: School Days

High School Career

After graduating from Washington Junior High School in 1935, Jackie Robinson went on to attend John Muir Technical High School in Pasadena, California. It was the same school that his older brother Mack attended and graduated from. The year following his graduation, Mack represented the United States in the Berlin Olympics and won the silver medal in track and field. It was his family's accomplishments and encouragement that ultimately persuaded Jackie Robinson to pursue the life of an athlete.

In most cases, African Americans at that time had to choose between life on the streets or the life of a low-level employee working for a salary lower than their white counterparts were making. But Jackie had another choice because of his athletic prowess. He made the decision to work his butt off to excel as an athlete, realizing that he basically had nowhere else to go as far as a career was concerned.

Spending his entire high school career as an athlete, Jackie Robinson poured his energy into working hard in all of the sports he played. We know him as someone who stood out as a professional baseball player later in his career, but he was already so good an athlete back at Muir Tech that he was able to perform remarkably well in five different sports.

Robinson played shortstop and also catcher when he starred for his high school's baseball team. Then, as a football player, Jackie performed well as the team's quarterback. In basketball, he also showed off his athletic giftedness and natural feel for sports by playing both guard and forward for the varsity team. He also went on to perform just as well as his brother did in track and field when he won several awards in the broad jump. Jackie Robinson even excelled in tennis and went on to win the Pacific Coast Negro

Tennis Tournament back in 1936. The young man lettered in baseball, football, basketball, and track and field, demonstrating how good an athlete he really was even when he was still in high school.[iv]

It was an understatement to say that Jackie Robinson was one of the best young athletes in all of California at that time. In fact, he was so good that in 1937 the *Pasadena Star-News* reported that Robinson was Muir's best athlete in the two years he spent with the school.[iv] The newspaper did not care about Robinson's color and still described him as the school's best athlete, even though he was playing for teams mainly composed of white athletes. In that regard, no other young man in his high school was as gifted as he was at that time.

Junior College Career

Finishing his studies after two years at Muir Tech, Jackie Robinson's athletic prowess did not end when he went on to attend Pasadena Junior College immediately after graduating from high school. He continued to excel in all of the four major sports he played when he was in high school. At Pasadena Junior College (PJC), he was still one of the better athletes in baseball, football, basketball, and track and field.

In baseball, he continued to play shortstop. Meanwhile, in football, he was still a quarterback but also spent time at safety for PJC. At that time, Robinson's favored sport was actually football instead of baseball, even though he is now obviously better known for his baseball career. He even went on to break his school's records for the broad jump competition when he played for the track and field team. It was in 1938 when he had a broad jump record of 25 feet, 6-1/2 inches at the Southern California Junior College track meet.[v]

Sometime during his days with Pasadena Junior College, Jackie Robinson broke an ankle while playing football. While the broken ankle did not derail his career as a standout athlete, the injury eventually led to complications that delayed his life of service in the United States military. Some would even say that, had he not broken his ankle, Robinson would not have chosen baseball over football. At that time, Jackie was fonder of football; he did not play a lot of baseball save for the time he played a few games for the Pasadena Sox, sometime between 1938 and 1939.[v] Had he not broken his ankle, we might be talking about Jackie Robinson today as a football player rather than a baseball star. Regardless of that, he was so gifted an athlete that he would surely have risen up as a star even if he did indeed choose to play football instead.

It was during his time with PJC that Jackie Robinson began to manifest his stance of non-tolerance against racist authority figures. In 1938, he had a vocal dispute against policemen who had detained one of his friends, a black American. The incident led to his arrest and eventually gave Robinson a reputation as someone who was not afraid to hold his ground against racism and those who practiced it.[iv] Robinson's antagonistic personality against the ill effects of racism never wavered from then on, as he simply continued to fight for his rights on behalf of all the African Americans of his time.

Tragedy struck when Jackie Robinson was still in Pasadena Junior College. Just when he was about to finish his studies at PJC, his brother Frank was killed in a motorcycle accident. Frank was the brother Jackie was closest to back in those days and was one of the main figures that had convinced him to pursue the life of an athlete when he was still in high school. Frank's death only solidified his resolve, as Jackie was motivated to honor his brother's name by continuing his life as an athlete when he went to college after graduating from PJC.[iii]

College Career

After finishing his studies with PJC, Jackie Robinson went on to enroll at the University of California, Los Angeles (UCLA) to stay close to home while continuing his pursuit of the life of a standout athlete. Again, Robinson stood out in baseball, football, basketball, and track and field when he was at UCLA. However, he was still more focused on football at that time.

Robinson's days with the UCLA Bruins were not indicative of his future career as one of the greatest figures in the history of baseball. He was a productive forward for his school's basketball team, but he stood out more in football. Jackie was only one of four black players on his football team at UCLA. Three of those black players played backfield positions for the Bruins. Robinson helped UCLA win six games, with no losses in the 10 games they played. They tied four times that season.

Performing amazingly well for his school's track and field team, Jackie Robinson went on to win the 1940 NCAA title in the long jump when he recorded a jump of over twenty-four feet (24 feet, 1 and ¼ of an inch to be exact). Oddly enough, his worst sport back in UCLA was baseball, as he had a batting average of only .097, which was poor for any kind of hitter.[vi] Nevertheless, he still displayed the quickness that allowed him to perform well whenever he was stealing home plate and was able to go for 19 of those steals in his entire career at UCLA. But at that point, no one thought that Jackie Robinson was going to be a baseball player, or even one of the greatest players in baseball, because of how poorly he played when he was still with the Bruins.

During the spring of his senior year in college, Jackie Robinson made an important career move that changed his life. Things were not easy for Robinson and his family during those days. Financial struggles forced him to quit school, even though he was nearing graduation. He needed a job to help his family with expenses. As such, he was able to land a job at the National Youth Administration as an assistant athletic director.

When the United States discontinued the NYA's operations, Robinson moved far away to Honolulu, Hawaii to seek the life of a football player. There, he played for a semi-professional team called the Honolulu Bears, which was racially integrated. But he did not last long in Hawaii, and he eventually moved back to California to play running back for the Los Angeles Bulldogs, another semi-professional team that played for the Pacific Coast Football League. But things changed when World War II began, as Jackie Robinson's football career abruptly came to an end.

Chapter 3: Military Service

When the Japanese attacked Pearl Harbor, the United States was dragged into World War II and several young men were either forced to enlist or were drafted into the military. In Jackie Robinson's case, he was drafted into the Army in 1942 and was forced to drop his career as a football player. He was stationed in Fort Riley, Kansas at that time and never saw combat during the entire tenure of his military service.

Shortly after getting drafted, Jackie Robinson tried his hand at the Officer Candidate School because he did indeed have the qualifications that would allow him to do so. It also helped that, in the 1941 OCS guidelines, the qualifications were race-neutral. Nevertheless, because whites still did not see their black counterparts as equals, even in the middle of a great war, only a few black applicants were accepted into the OCS.

Meanwhile, Jackie Robinson might not have been rejected outright, but his OCS application was noticeably delayed in comparison to the processing time of white applicants. Luckily for Robinson and his other black applicants, they had the help of Joe Louis, one of the greatest boxing heavyweight champions of all time. Louis was also stationed in Fort Riley at that time and was friends with lawyer Truman Gibson, who worked as a civilian aide for the US Secretary of War. Because Louis and Gibson were already friends before the war, the heavyweight champion was able to facilitate the OCS applications of several black Americans, including Jackie Robinson's.[iv] Because of that, Robinson and Louis started a friendship that would transcend their time together in Fort Riley.

Jackie Robinson successfully finished OCS and was commissioned as a second lieutenant in January of 1943 while the war still waged on. He was later reassigned to Fort Hood, Texas after receiving his commission as an officer. However, Robinson did not have the most agreeable time while he was serving in the military due to another episode of racism.

On July 6, 1944, Jackie Robinson boarded an Army bus and was asked by the driver to move to the back of the bus, even though the Army had previously commissioned an unsegregated bus line. Knowing for certain what his rights were, Jackie Robinson refused. And while the bus driver initially backed down after Robinson refused his demand, he eventually called for military police to take the second lieutenant into custody for his refusal.[vii]

Jackie Robinson did not back down from the military police. He confronted them for their racist acts and was eventually recommended to get court-martialed. Supporting Robinson, the commander of the battalion to which Robinson was assigned refused to authorize the action against the second lieutenant. After that, Robinson was suddenly transferred to a different battalion whose commander was quick to authorize the legal action against Jackie. He was court-martialed for acts he did not commit—including public drunkenness, despite the fact that Jackie Robinson was known to be someone who did not drink.[vii]

Jackie Robinson's court proceedings prevented him from getting deployed on the field when his original battalion was sent to see combat action. He was never able to properly serve his country as a combatant in World War II due to those proceedings, but luckily for him, he was acquitted by a panel that was composed of nine white officers.[vii] It was an experience that Jackie Robinson would never forget, as it allowed him to become someone who stayed strong in the fight against racism and segregation.

That was not the only episode of racism that Jackie Robinson encountered while he was serving in the Army. Sports have always been one of the more important parts of life in the military and it was normal for college standouts to get drafted. Different teams in the military are often very competitive, regardless of the sport they played. Knowing that Robinson played football when he was in college, the military tried to recruit him over to Fort Riley's football team back when Jackie was still stationed there.[vii] Jackie refused because he had other plans in mind—he wanted to play for Fort Riley's baseball team.

Pete Reiser, who eventually became Robinson's MLB teammate, was also serving at Fort Riley at the time. He did not know who Robinson was back then, but he remembered how the Fort Riley baseball team humiliated the young man. Jackie wanted to try out for the team, but he was turned down by the officer in charge because he "should be playing for the colored team instead." However, there was no colored team in Fort Riley! At first, Robinson stood there watching the team that had rejected him, knowing for a fact that he had been turned down in the most humiliating fashion. However, he could not do anything and simply walked away instead. He still turned down the chance to play for the football team because what he wanted to do at that time was play baseball.[vii]

After Jackie Robinson was acquitted of his charges, he was eventually transferred to Kentucky, where he was asked to coach the Army sports teams. It was there where Robinson met a former player who played for the Kansas City Monarchs of the baseball Negro American League. His newfound friend told him to ask for a tryout for the team. Robinson did so after he was honorably discharged from his military service in November of 1944.

Chapter 4: Pre-MLB Career

The Negro League

After his military service, Jackie Robinson spent some time with the Los Angeles Bulldogs before accepting an offer to serve as the athletic director for Samuel Huston College in Austin, Texas. He was tasked to serve as the team's basketball coach, but he struggled to find players who would suit up for him because the club was still in its early stages. At times, he even had to play for the team in exhibition games because of their lack of players.

While he was still working for Samuel Huston College, the Kansas City Monarchs, the team he wrote to for a tryout after his military service, offered him a chance to play professional baseball for them in the Negro League. The offer was for a paycheck worth $400 a month, which Jackie Robinson promptly accepted. He was on his way to Kansas City to start his journey as a baseball player.

There was no doubt that Jackie Robinson had a pretty fruitful career when he was still playing for the Kansas City Monarchs. He played well enough to eventually catch the attention of the big names in the MLB. However, he did not exactly love the experience. The Negro League was not as structured as other professional baseball teams and was not even as well-organized as the environment Jackie had experienced back in college. For the most part, the Negro League was a league designed to give the MLB a reason for the color barrier. It was the perfect excuse, as they could always point towards the Negro League whenever a black American tried to enter the MLB. As such, the Negro League became a place where talented athletes were wasted and where gambling proliferated.

In the single season Jackie Robinson spent with the Kansas City Monarchs, he played 47 games at shortstop and had an impressive .387 batting average, which was way above his batting average when he was in college. He also finished with five home runs and showed his aptitude as a base stealer after recording a total of 13 stolen bases.

During that season, Jackie Robinson performed so well that he attracted the attention of the MLB at a time when the color line was yet to be crossed. Back then, there were no black players in the MLB—teams continued to adhere to the color barrier, a policy of exclusion which had existed since the beginning of the 1900s. There were no official rules stating that black players were not allowed to enter the MLB, but team owners had an unwritten agreement amongst themselves to prevent the entry of African American players and other players of color into their teams. The last black American to play in the MLB was way back during the 1880s. Since then, the color barrier was in full effect and no black player was able to break it no matter how good they were.

Things seemingly started to change when the Boston Red Sox held a tryout for Jackie Robinson and several other black players in the famous Fenway Park. However, the tryout turned out to be merely an exhibition, as the Red Sox actually had no interest in signing an African American into their roster. It was believed that the tryout was just a spectacle orchestrated to please a city councilman who was opposed to the idea of the color barrier in the MLB. Indeed, the Red Sox eventually turned out to be the most racially discriminating team at that time, as it took them until 1959 to allow black players to play for the team. They were the final MLB team to fully integrate people of color into the roster.[viii]

Instead of making it to an MLB roster by trying out for the Red Sox, Jackie Robinson left Fenway Park humiliated. He was subjected to racial epithets even though it was a closed-door tryout that only had team managers and executives sitting on the bleachers. At that point, it was becoming clear that the MLB and the people running the league were not ready to embrace racial integration. The color barrier still seemed unbreakable.

Meeting with Branch Rickey

When Jackie Robinson and other black players were losing hope of one day making it to the MLB, one man was more than serious enough to actually want to integrate his roster by adding a black player. That man was Branch Rickey, the man running the show for the Brooklyn Dodgers.

Unlike the other owners and team managers in the MLB, Branch Rickey did not care about the unwritten color barrier rule. He wanted to add a black man to his team not because he was seeking a gimmick to make the team more popular, but because he really thought that black athletes were good enough to make the Brooklyn Dodgers better and more competitive. To this end, he thoroughly scouted the Negro League to look for a suitable candidate for the single roster spot he was willing to give to a black American player.

At that time, Jackie Robinson was already a well-known name in the country because of his bravery in standing up to military officials during his time in the Army. Branch Rickey thought that Robinson was a suitable player to carry over to the MLB because of his amazing athletic gifts and his ability to stand up for himself against racist jeers.

Rickey and Robinson officially held a one-on-one meeting on August 18, 1945, to discuss the future of the former second lieutenant. Some people today consider the meeting a trivial formality, but it was actually a meeting that undoubtedly changed the landscape of the MLB and brought about a rippling effect that transformed the entire world. Nobody at that time knew that a three-hour session between two sports personalities would have an effect that would last for decades and possibly even centuries.

It was crucial that Rickey got to meet Robinson and talk to him to learn more about the man and his personality. The Brooklyn Dodgers general manager was not just looking for an African American player who had the talent and athleticism that could elevate the team's overall play—if that was the case, the Negro League was full of players who were just as athletically gifted as Jackie. Instead, what Rickey wanted was someone he thought could bear the constant verbal abuse and the pressure that comes with being the first black player in the modern-day version of the MLB.

In that famous conversation between Rickey and Robinson, the one thing that stood out the most was the former asking the latter if he was someone who could play for years in the MLB while absorbing all of the racial insults thrown at him. After all, Branch Rickey knew for a fact that Jackie Robinson had a history of confronting authority figures and those whom he perceived were racist towards him and his fellow black Americans. To that, Robinson asked Rickey if he was looking for a black player who was afraid to fight back. But the general manager simply answered that he wanted someone strong enough to turn the other cheek and be the better man in the middle of racial antagonism.[viii]

It was at that moment that Jackie Robinson's life changed. Already known for being the black man who stood up to military officials, Robinson had a reputation for being someone who would rather angrily retaliate and fight back against racism. But that conversation with Rickey allowed him to reflect back and realize that angry retaliation was not the best way to fight against the oppression that he and his fellow black Americans were facing during that period in history. He committed to Rickey, affirming that he was going to be someone who would rather turn the other cheek and absorb all of the negativity instead of fighting back. On November 1, 1945, Robinson formally committed to a contract that would pay him a $600 monthly salary. It was also announced that he was going to be playing for the Montreal Royals, the

Dodgers' farm club in the International League, during the 1946 season.

While it was a shocker to the entire world that Jackie Robinson was set to become the first black player in the International League since the 1800s, the decision did not exactly sit well with some of the players in the Negro League even though the move to sign the former second lieutenant paved the way for black players to start entering the MLB. There was a belief that no matter how athletically gifted and talented Jackie Robinson was, he was not the best player in the Negro League at the time. Josh Gibson, who had never made it to the MLB as he fell into a coma in 1943 and died early in 1947, was actually better than any other black player back then, yet no MLB team had been interested in signing him to a contract. Some even said that Robinson's Monarchs teammate Satchel Paige was also the better player.[ix]

Nevertheless, Jackie Robinson was there to break the color barrier, not to proclaim to the world that he was the best player coming out of the Negro League. After all, Rickey signed him not because he thought he was the best, but because Jackie was someone he thought was the best choice to usher in a new generation of black players making their way to the MLB.

The Minor Leagues

As announced, Jackie Robinson went on to join the Montreal Royals in Florida for spring training in preparation for the 1946 AAA International League. However, even though he had been sent there by Branch Rickey, he still encountered some problems with team manager Clay Hopper, who viewed black Americans differently at that time. He asked Rickey to assign Robinson to another team, a request that the general manager declined. But, fortunately, Hopper changed his views on racism after working with Jackie Robinson, who went on to say that the team's manager actually treated all of his players equally, regardless of color and race.[x]

While Clay Hopper may have changed his views later on, it was a turbulent start for him. Aside from requesting that Robinson be moved to another team, Hopper commented that his father, had he still been alive, would have been disappointed to see him managing a black player. He even went so far as to say that Robinson was not a human being when Branch Rickey exclaimed at an amazing play that Jackie had made during spring training. But Rickey did not try to convince Hopper to change his views with his words. Clay Hopper, a man born in the South where racism was at its peak, was simply a product of the bigotry of his generation.[x] Instead, Rickey wanted Hopper to change his views by spending time with the remarkable Jackie Robinson.

Over the course of spring training, Robinson still struggled against racism. He was not even allowed to stay in the same hotel as his white teammates, as the state of Florida was still at the height of its racist views against people of color. Instead, Jackie had to lodge at the home of an African American couple who lived close by. There were also issues regarding Robinson's presence in the training facility, which the Dodgers did not own. The police chief of Sanford, Florida threatened to cancel the Royals' games if they allowed Jackie Robinson to play. And in Jacksonville, the stadium was padlocked without prior notice to the Royals because they said that the locals did not want to see a black man such as Robinson playing there.[xi]

Because of scheduling issues and problems with how city officials viewed the Royals and Jackie Robinson, the first black player in the International League since the 1880s could not even play his first official minor league game until March 17th of that year. However, Rickey was adamant in making sure that Robinson was going to be able to play. He tried his best to lobby with local officials to let the Royals play even with Jackie on the roster. As such, Robinson was finally able to play on March 17, 1946, against the Brooklyn Dodgers in Daytona Beach. Jackie Robinson became the first player to suit up for a minor league club since the 1880s.

Jackie Robinson made his first true minor league appearance on April 18, 1946, when the Royals met the Jersey City Giants. In Robinson's first at-bat, the pitcher he went up against was Warren Sandel, who had already known how good an athlete Jackie was because they both played against one another in their home state of California. Sandel respected Robinson's game and his talent as an athlete and refused to pitch the ball right at him even though his superiors requested that he do so. Instead, Sandel pitched fairly—and Jackie Robinson ended up dominating by going for four hits in just his first five at-bats. The Royals handily won that game 14-1 on the strength of Jackie Robinson's athletic prowess.

Jackie Robinson impressed the entire baseball world during his first season playing in the minor league. However, it was incredibly difficult for him to actually play in a league that white Americans believed should only be theirs. The Royals often faced hostile conditions when they were traveling to other cities to play opposing teams. At one point, the team had to cancel one of their tours in the South due to the hostile environment awaiting Robinson there.

Regardless of how fans of opposing teams jeered and hurled racial insults towards him, Jackie Robinson had the support of the Montreal faithful because Canadians were not as opposed to breaking the color barrier in baseball as some Americans were at that time.[xii] He got a lot of love from fans and Robinson was the reason why the Montreal Royals were the most popular International League team at that time.[xiii] It did not matter whether or not fans were there to cheer him on because the stadiums were always full whenever Jackie was there to play. Fellow African Americans were there to see the man who would soon break the MLB's color barrier. Meanwhile, those who were against racial integration in the MLB were there to make sure Robinson heard their hatred.

In actuality, Jackie Robinson did not mind, as he soon adjusted to all of the insults as well as to the cheers he received. He was the International League's best player that season when he led the league with a .349 batting average and a .985 fielding percentage. Robinson was rightfully named the league MVP and was the first black player to receive such a prestigious award from the minor leagues. But, most importantly, the Royals went on to win the league championship that season.

As Jackie Robinson played his heart out for the Montreal Royals and made it known to everyone that he had the talent to make it to the MLB, he made a believer out of team manager Clay Hopper. Formerly someone who was always against racial integration in the MLB because of his upbringing in the South, Hopper became an enthusiastic believer in Jackie Robinson. When the Royals won the championship, he went to Robinson, shook his hand, and told him that he was "a great ballplayer and a fine gentleman." It was also Hopper who recommended that Robinson be elevated to the Brooklynn Dodgers the following season. Jackie Robinson redeemed Clay Hopper, who was one of the first persons he helped change his views on racial integration.[x]

Chapter 5: MLB Career

Breaking the Color Barrier

Just six days before the start of the 1947 MLB season, Jackie Robinson was elevated to the Brooklyn Dodgers after Montreal Monarchs team manager Clay Hopper endorsed and recommended the 1946 International MVP get promoted to the main team. Playing shortstop back when he was still in the Negro League, Robinson was eventually moved to second base in Montreal but was set to play first base in Brooklyn because the Dodgers already had a starting second baseman in Eddie Stanky. It was also the only remaining position left on the roster.[xiv] Regardless of what position he played on the field, Jackie Robinson was going to make history.

It was on April 15, 1947, when the 28-year-old Jackie Robinson made his official MLB debut. At long last, the color barrier than had not been breached since 1884 was finally broken, as Robinson was the first black player to play for an MLB team since then. His dream of making a statement by playing in the MLB and Branch Rickey's aspirations of getting a black player to help his Brooklyn Dodgers were now fulfilled. In front of a crowd of over 26,000, which was composed of more than 14,000 black fans, Robinson helped his team win 5-3.

It was described that the Jackie Robinson Brooklyn Dodgers debut in Brooklyn, New York, was the most anticipated game in the history of the entire sport. That was because it represented two sides of the coin at that point in time. The heads side represented the black Americans who were longing for an equal opportunity to play in the MLB and were beginning to regain hope as Jackie made it possible for them. Meanwhile, the tails side represented the fear of traditional white Americans who still clung to the idea of racial segregation. Regardless of how Americans viewed that game, it was clear that Jackie Robinson's official debut was the start of something new, not only in the game of baseball but also in the history of mankind itself.[xiv]

The season progressed and it was clear that the media had mixed reactions to Jackie Robinson's promotion to the MLB, but it was nevertheless more positive than negative. Robinson also had to adjust to playing first base that season after spending a lot of time as a shortstop and at second base. However, that was the least of his struggles when he first came to the MLB.

While millions of fans around the country rejoiced in the fact that the color barrier had finally been broken by one of the game's finest players, it was not all rainbows and butterflies in the Brooklyn Dodgers' roster. Robinson might have already been a part of the team, but there were still Dodgers who did not see eye to eye with the management's decision to bring over a black man from the Negro League. Some of the players tried to form an uprising against Robinson and team management by threatening to sit out games rather than play alongside a black player.[xv] There was turmoil in the Brooklyn Dodgers' locker room even though they were actually winning games with Robinson helping them. For some players, their pride and their obsolete belief that they were superior to black Americans were getting in the way of what was more important.

Seeing things from a bigger perspective, team management took Jackie Robinson's side. The team manager, Leo Durocher, who shared Branch Rickey's views, made it clear to the Dodgers that he did not care what the player's color was because what mattered was his decision on who should play. Insinuating that Robinson was someone who could help them win and bring in the money, he told his players that those who were not willing to play would be traded. This effectively silenced the plans of mutiny that could have very well sidelined the Brooklyn Dodger's season.

Problems with him being on the team were over, but Jackie Robinson and the Brooklyn Dodgers still had to contend with the fact that other teams all over the league were not ready to accept a black man playing in the MLB. There was a rumor of a plot by the St. Louis Cardinals to go on a strike against the Brooklyn Dodgers and try to spread their cause throughout the entire league. The leak was rumored to have come from the Cardinals' physician, who told the news to his friends in the media. In turn, the media printed it in newspapers and it became a national headline.

To that end, it reached National League president Ford Frick's office and got the attention of Baseball Commissioner Happy Chandler; both Frick and Chandler made it clear that anyone who wanted to go on strike against the Dodgers to make a statement against Jackie Robinson would be suspended. The league officials effectively took Jackie's side and even went on to say that they would try their best to make sure that media outlets did not take the side of those who were against Robinson and that they did not care if suspending players hampered the league's operations for a handful of years. It was becoming obvious that Jackie Robinson had made believers out of the MLB's highest officials and was changing racial views from the top.

While the Cardinals denied the allegation that they were planning a strike, Jackie Robinson changed the views of not only the league officials but sports media as well. Even sports publications that were previously in support of the color line had changed their views and began supporting Jackie Robinson's presence in the MLB. And while talks had been silenced about a strike and how other teams were not really in agreement with Jackie playing in the MLB, it was still difficult to make believers out of players and fans alike.

Some of the players who were still in support of racial segregation made it difficult for Jackie Robinson all season long. Opposing players were treating Robinson unfairly rough during games to the point that he even received a gash on his leg due to one of the physical plays from an opposing player.[xvi] One time, when the Dodgers played the Philadelphia Phillies, Robinson was the victim of racial insults from the team manager, who told him that "he should go back to the cotton fields." To this end, Robinson later said that those insults against him only served to help unite the Brooklyn Dodgers, as he and his teammates went on to retaliate against any forms of abuse by playing their hardest on the field instead of getting back at them in the same manner.

But things were not always grim for Robinson when it came to how opposing players viewed his presence in the league. It may have been true that a lot of white players were against breaking the color barrier, but there were notable names who gave their support to Jackie Robinson. Lee "Jeep" Handley, who was with the Philadelphia Phillies at that time, was one of the first names that Robinson mentioned when he was asked about who was concerned about him. Pee Wee Reese, one of Robinson's best friends on the Dodgers team, once said a famous line that goes "You can hate a man for many reasons. Color is not one of them."[xvii] And whenever fans were verbally abusing Jackie Robinson, it was said that Reese would always put his arm around his good friend to try to defend the man from all of the hatred he was getting. And Jewish baseball player Hank Greenberg, who also received his fair share of insults from players and fans alike, told Robinson that the best way to defeat his haters was to actually beat them in games.[xviii]

Jackie Robinson ended up playing a total of 151 games that season while he was battling racial insults and antagonistic views from players and fans alike. He had a lot on his plate, but he still managed to focus on the task at hand by playing well for the team, and he was probably the best player on the Dodgers' roster that season. He led the team in runs and hits with 125 and 175 respectively. He also led the league with 28 stolen bases and 28 sacrifice hits. Jackie also finished with batting stats of .297, .383, and .427. Dominating the league in his first year with the Dodgers, Jackie Robinson was named the MLB's first-ever Rookie of the Year. He even went on to finish fifth in the MVP race that season.

More importantly, Jackie Robinson was the major reason why the Brooklyn Dodgers were gaining enough support from fans and the media to play at their best. The team led the National League in wins at the end of the regular season and even went on to play the New York Yankees in the World Series. In what was a hard-fought championship series against the Yankees, the Brooklyn Dodgers ended up losing to their crosstown rivals in seven games. While the Dodgers may not have won it all that season, having Robinson on the roster was a win for them, the African American community, and humanity as a whole.

But breaking the color barrier was only the first step for Jackie Robinson. He was not there to just be a mere novelty in the MLB, but was in the league to prove that he still had a lot of work to do before the world was ready to treat black men as equals, not only in sports but outside of it as well. Robinson was going to be a force in the entire league for years to come. And just like how the MLB was not yet ready for a black man to start dominating them, they were not ready for what Jackie Robinson was going to bring in the next few seasons.

Influx of Black Players, Easing Pressure

Jackie Robinson, after surprising the entire world and proving his worth as a baseball player in just his first MLB season, went on to earn himself a salary raise and signed a contract worth $12,000. Plus, he managed to earn even more when he became a huge celebrity during the offseason, joining a vaudeville tour to the South, which normally is not very receptive to people of color. During his tour, Robinson had to undergo ankle surgery in preparation for the 1948 baseball season.

Enjoying himself too much during the offseason and focusing more on his activities at that time, Jackie Robinson came to spring training 30 pounds heavier than normal. The bad part was that the weight he gained was unhealthy. Robinson had to lose all of that weight during spring training but losing weight and cutting down on food left him weaker than he was during his rookie season. This certainly prevented Jackie from taking a huge step in his second season in the league, but he was still as productive as he was a year ago.

After playing his rookie year at first base, Robinson was eventually moved to second base when Stanky was traded to the Boston Braves. This allowed Jackie to move back to his natural position, but he still played first base from time to time, depending on what the

Brooklyn Dodgers needed from him in certain situations that season.

Jackie Robinson went on to play 147 games the entire season and led the Brooklyn Dodgers to third place in the National League after winning 84 total games. He had a total of 108 runs and 170 hits that season. However, Robinson regressed in some aspects of his game, as he finished with 22 stolen bases and a total of only 8 sacrifice hits, which were 20 hits lower than his previous season. His batting averages of .296, .367, and .453 were similar to the ones he had a year ago. However, he still managed to have a .980 fielding percentage, which was good for second in the National League, only behind former teammate Eddie Stanky.

A year removed from losing to the New York Yankees in the World Series, the Brooklyn Dodgers could not make a return trip to the championship series when they could not best the Boston Braves, who went on to win the National League Championship but lost to the

Cleveland Indians in the 1948 World Series. Oddly enough, Jackie Robinson was not the first black player to win a World Series title, as the Cleveland Indians were also responsible for bringing in quality African American players into their roster.

Jackie Robinson was the first to break the color barrier, but he was not alone when he did so. Larry Doby followed shortly thereafter, becoming the first American League black player when he came into the MLB just eleven weeks after Robinson made his official debut in 1947. And the 42-year-old Satchel Paige, who was one of the best players in the history of the Negro League, became the oldest player to make it to the MLB in 1948. Both Doby and Paige were signed by the Cleveland Indians. Meanwhile, the Brooklyn Dodgers also went on to sign three more black players in 1948.

While both Doby and Paige were the first black players to win a World Series Championship since the color barrier was broken, it was Jackie Robinson who paved the way for his fellow African Americans to make it to the MLB. More importantly, it was also Robinson who absorbed all of the negativity and the media attention during his first year in the league to make it easier for his fellow black players to make the transition to the MLB. In that sense, Robinson may not have been the first to win a title, but he was still the most important black American player in the entire league at that point in history.

However, it is also important to note that having more black players in the league also helped Robinson in the same way that he helped his fellow African Americans. Considering the fact that there were more and more black players entering the MLB in 1948 and beyond, people were not as hard on Robinson as they were in the past. The fans of the sport, regardless of whether or not they supported racial integration in the league, were beginning to accept the fact that black players were already going to be a part of the MLB heading into the future. More importantly, more and more haters were also beginning to transform into believers after seeing what Robinson, Doby, and Paige were capable of doing. The influx of black players that season made it much more comfortable for MLB teams to try to sign African Americans.

MVP Season

Jackie Robinson may have had a good second year in the MLB, but he was visibly weaker at the plate than he was in his rookie year because he lost a lot of weight as well as power when he underwent strict dieting during the spring of 1948. As such, his batting stats were not quite as impressive as what he had in his rookie year, but he still maintained numbers good enough to prove his talents as a standout athlete. But being good was not enough for Robinson.

It was during the spring of 1949 when Jackie Robinson went on to seek the help of Hall of Famer George Sisler to improve his performance as a hitter.[xix]   The decision to seek the help of one of the greatest players in the history of the league was what allowed Robinson to improve drastically that year and to make the leap from being a good player to being one of the greats in the entire MLB that season.

Jackie Robinson remembered how Sisler, who was working as an adviser to the Dodgers at that time, improved his hitting technique at the plate. One of the things that Sisler taught Robinson was how to make sure that the ball goes to the right field after hitting it. On top of that, he taught Jackie that power was not always the most important factor when batting, as he also needed to learn how to counter certain pitches, such as the fastball, on the belief that it was going to be easier for him to learn how to adjust to hitting a curveball. Meanwhile, his form also needed some refinement, and Jackie learned how to stand upright and check his swing even at the last moment whenever he was on the plate and about to hit a ball.[xix]

The work that Jackie Robinson put himself through during the entire offseason paid dividends throughout the 1949 MLB season. Robinson seemed like an entirely different breed of athlete whenever he was on the plate. Everyone already knew how remarkable of a player he was, but Robinson took his game to the next level with the help of Sisler. He was not only a powerful hitter but was also an extremely accurate one throughout the entire season as pitchers had no answer for Robinson, who seemingly knew how to counter every type of ball thrown right at him.

Jackie Robinson was so popular and was so good at hitting the ball that season that the song "Did You See Jackie Robinson Hit That Ball?" written and performed by Buddy Johnson climbed as high as 13th on the music charts that year.[xx] On top of that, Robinson's popularity got him voted by fans into the 1949 MLB All-Star Game as the starting second baseman.

While it was natural for his fellow black Americans to vote for him, Robinson's popularity reached heights that turned former supporters of the color barrier into believers. Jackie did not only literally break the color barrier but also helped in convincing all kinds of fans that it was alright for a person of color to be in the MLB. Jackie Robinson went on to become the headliner of the first MLB All-Star Game to feature black players.[xxi] The game also included Larry Doby, Roy Campanella, and Don Newcombe.

At the end of the regular season, Jackie Robinson led the league with a batting average of .342, proving that his technique and refinement at hitting the ball were at an all-time high because of his training during the offseason. Moreover, he also led the league with 37 stolen bases and 17 sacrifice hits on top of the 122 runs, 203 hits, and 16 home runs he had in the 156 games he played for the Brooklyn Dodgers. He led the Dodgers to the top of the National League standings with 97 total wins. Because of that and his overall improvement as a star baseball player, Jackie Robinson became the first-ever black athlete to win the National League MVP. Meanwhile, it was only in 1963 when Elston Howard became the first black American League MVP.

Jackie Robinson led the Brooklyn Dodgers to the World Series for the second time in a span of three years. They once again met their crosstown rivals, the New York Yankees, in the grandest baseball stage of them all. However, the Yankees ended up defeating the Dodgers in five games to leave Robinson without a World Series title in the three years he had spent in the MLB.

Although Robinson's 1949 season was his most fruitful as a baseball player, he experienced one of the biggest distractions he had ever had in his life when he was asked to testify before the US House of Representatives' Committee on Un-American Activities concerning what was perceived to be a dangerous statement made by fellow black American Paul Robeson, who was alleged to have said something against the United States in the middle of the Cold War.

Jackie Robinson was in the middle of a dilemma of sorts when he was asked to testify in front of Congress. Paul Robeson had a direct positive effect on his baseball career because he was one of the many outspoken civil rights activists who helped pave the way for racial integration in baseball. It was in December of 1943 when Robeson spoke in front of MLB team owners in relation to how they should start integrating black players because baseball was a national sport that should be enjoyed by everyone in the country.[xxii] After Robeson's speech, the commissioner at that time reiterated that there was nothing in the rule book that prevented black players from entering the MLB. As such, this paved the way for Jackie Robinson to enter the league as the first black player in the MLB's modern period.[xxiii]

As such, it was a struggle for Jackie Robinson to go and testify against the man who helped make it possible for him to achieve something that no other African American had achieved in the past. However, he also thought that declining to testify would affect his baseball career and the progression of black integration in baseball and other major sports. In front of the Congress, Robinson went on to say that Robeson's statements were a product of his free and personal views, but he still made it a point to say that, no matter how true Robeson's statements were regarding how blacks were seemingly treated better by Communists than they were by Americans, it still did not change how "un-American" his statements were.[xxiv]

The reactions of the black press were mixed even though much of the other major news outlets all over the country were in favor of Robinson's statements. While there were some newspapers that said Robinson was a scared dog who was afraid of how America would treat him had he agreed with Robeson's "un-

American" statements, it was clear that Jackie's words still had positive results regarding the political nature of the Cold War and how Robeson could possibly sway black Americans over to the Communist way of thinking. Regardless of the effects of his statements, Robinson went on to have a deep admiration for Robeson when the latter declined to comment negatively on what the baseball star had said in front of Congress.

Outside Interests, Continuing to Contend

Jackie Robinson may have been a baseball player, but he was first and foremost an African American trying to lift himself up in a society that viewed black people differently. In line with that, he allowed himself to pursue interests outside of baseball in the hopes of not only trying to make a living for himself (he was getting paid $35,000, the highest mark a Dodgers player had at that point in history) but also to try to make a statement.

It was in 1950 when Jackie Robinson's film biography was released. What was unusual about that film was that Robinson played himself, even though he was still in the middle of a busy schedule as a baseball player. The film allowed him to have a stage where he could help inspire other black Americans to rise up in a society that did not treat them as equals. Simply telling his full story was enough to give his fellow black people hope that they would also one day reach the heights that Robinson had reached at that point in his career.

While Jackie Robinson may have helped inspire millions of people with his film biography and exploits as a personality in Hollywood, it changed the relationship between Branch Rickey and team co-owner Walter O'Malley, who called the 1949 National League MVP "Rickey's prima donna." This eventually led to Rickey leaving the team for good after his contract as the team's president expired in 1950. He later cashed in his ownership of the franchise to give

O'Malley full control over the Brooklyn Dodgers after the two could no longer see eye to eye in the middle of Jackie Robinson's rise to fame as a superstar. Robinson later penned a letter addressed to Rickey thanking him for everything he had done for him as the father figure he had never had while he was growing up.[xxv]

Nevertheless, Jackie Robinson remained one of the best players in the league that season and was once again an All-Star even though he did not have a year that was similar to that of his MVP season. He led the league in double plays made by a player at his position while also finishing with a .328 batting average, 99 runs, and 170 hits in the 144 games he played that year. The Dodgers finished second in the National League that season.

In the following season, Jackie Robinson was the one leading the Brooklyn Dodgers for another chance at contending for the National League pennant. Without the "distractions" he had a year ago as he was not working on a movie that season, Robinson had performances that were similar to when he won the MVP two years prior. He was the leader in the entire National League in terms of double plays made by a player at his position while making sure that he was putting up terrific stats. He had 106 runs, 185 hits, and 25 stolen bases while averaging .338, which was pretty close to the .342 average he had during his MVP season. Robinson, in his third straight season as an All-Star, actually finished sixth for the National League MVP that season. More importantly, it was his terrific plays that allowed the Brooklyn Dodgers to contend for the pennant all year long.

It took until the final play of the regular season to decide who was going to the World Series to represent the National League. Jackie Robinson was the difference maker when he made a hit in the 13th inning. In the 14th inning, he was so clutch that he poured all he had into a single strike to hit a home run, which ultimately was the deciding factor in the entire game. Because of that win, the Brooklyn Dodgers were able to force a three-game series against the New York Giants to determine who was going to represent the National League.

The series went to a third and deciding game, which was one of the classics in the history of the sport. It took until the last at-bat of the New York Giants to determine who was going to the World Series. However, a home run by Bobby Thomson in the final at-bat ultimately buried the Dodgers' chances of winning the series. But while the entire stadium was shocked at the home run now known as the "Shot Heard 'Round the World," Jackie Robinson was the only player who was focused on what was happening, as he was watching Thomson's feet to make sure that he was indeed touching all bases after making that home run.[xxvi]

Even while slowly accepting his loss at the hands of Thomson, Robinson showed how much of a competitor he was by looking for any kind of technicality that could help them win what was already looking like a loss for the Dodgers. His competitive spirit was what kept him going when he first entered the MLB. Robinson was always someone who used his anger to fuel his fight for whatever he believed was right. That was what got him the attention of the entire nation when he fought back against military officials when he was with the Army. But, in the MLB, he could not use his anger because he had an agreement with Branch Rickey that he would turn the other cheek against any racial abuse he got from players and fans alike. Instead, he used his anger to fuel his competitive spirit, which gave way to the modern MLB version of Jackie Robinson instead of the angry and emotional second lieutenant that he was before he broke the color barrier.

The following season, Jackie Robinson went on to have what was another season close to his average. He was once again an All-Star and went on to have a .308 batting average on top of 104 runs and 157 hits while also finishing with a career-high on-base percentage of .440. But what appeared to be more important than Robinson's stats was how he helped his team improve during the regular season to finish with the National League pennant.

During the World Series, Jackie Robinson and his team once again fought against the New York Yankees, whom they could not beat in the previous two times that they made it to the World Series. This time, as before, they still could not beat the Yankees and the Brooklyn Dodgers went on to lose the World Series Championship to their rivals.

It was also that season when Jackie Robinson once again began to drift to other interests outside of baseball. In a television show where he made an appearance, he called out the New York Yankees for being one of the few remaining MLB teams that had yet to sign a black player since Robinson broke the color barrier in 1947. Meanwhile, he was also becoming too active in criticizing the media to the point that he called writer Dick Young a bigot. In response, the writer retaliated by saying that Jackie Robinson's biggest flaw as a person was that he believed everything bad that was happening to him at that point in his life was because of his color and not because of some of his actions.

A year later, Jackie Robinson also switched focus on the field by leaving the second base position for good. He was playing the first base, second base, third base, shortstop, and outfield positions during the 1953 season while giving the full-time second base to fellow black player Jim Gilliam. On top of that, he also went on to seek experience as a future major league team manager by trying to manage a team in the Puerto Rican Winter League. However, the MLB commissioner denied Robinson's outside interest in management.

That season, the 34-year-old Robinson was still an All-Star and finished with 109 runs, 159 hits, 17 stolen bases, and a batting average of .329. However, what ultimately made that season another failure for him and the Brooklyn Dodgers was their inability to defeat the New York Yankees in the World Series as the National League leaders were once again defeated by their rivals in the grandest stage in baseball.

Throughout 1953, Jackie Robinson did not only see some success on the field but also became much more active in his fight for civil rights. He was becoming more public when he was addressing racial issues and went on to criticize segregation in hotels, golf courses, and restaurants. To that end, more and more establishments started to open their doors to black Americans and became more integrated due to Robinson's fight against racial injustice. Jackie also became an editor for *Our Sports* magazine, which was known for tackling racial issues related to African Americans. Because Jackie Robinson was so successful in his fight against racial inequality, the baseball All-Star reportedly received a lot of death threats that year but he still was not deterred from trying to fight the good fight against how his fellow black Americans were getting treated in their own country.

Final All-Star Season, First and Only World Series Championship

During the 1954 season, Jackie Robinson started to show signs of wear and tear and the effects of his condition as a diabetic. On top of that, Robinson was also beginning to show the effects of his advancing age as he was no longer the same explosive and talented physical specimen that he was a few years back. Nevertheless, he was now eight years more experienced and wiser than he was when he first entered the league back in 1947. Robinson used his experience to his advantage though he still was not able to stay at his top physical state long enough to play more than 124 games that year.

While Robinson was still an All-Star, which was ultimately his final time, he finished with 62 runs and 120 hits while ending the season with a batting average of .311. That season, he was mostly playing the third base and the outfield, as Gilliam proved good enough to handle the second base on an everyday basis for the Brooklyn Dodgers. This time, however, the Brooklyn Dodgers failed to secure the National League pennant and ended up with the second place in the league after making two consecutive World Series appearances.

A year later, Jackie Robinson had the worst statistical season of his career. He was already 36 years old and was showing how much his skills and athletic capabilities had diminished. Entering his tenth season since breaking the color barrier, Robinson played for a

Brooklyn Dodgers team that already had enough talent to allow them to contend for the National League pennant once again. In the past, Jackie Robinson was undoubtedly the team's best player, but the Dodgers had learned to rely more on team effort rather than on the athletic prowess of their six-time All-Star.

Jackie Robinson finished the season playing a career-low 105 games and finished with career-low stats of 51 runs and 81 hits while ending the season with a batting average of .256. The Brooklyn Dodgers secured the National League pennant and met the New York Yankees in the World Series for the fifth time since Jackie Robinson joined the team in 1947.

The 1955 World Series reached a seventh and deciding game. However, Jackie Robinson was not even fielded in what was the deciding game in favor of the Brooklyn Dodgers. Team manager Walter Alston decided not to play his former All-Star player because he relied more on his younger players to win the

World Series for the Dodgers. While Jackie Robinson might not have played in the final game of the World Series, winning a championship for his team was what ultimately provided the punctuation he needed for what was already a historic career worthy of the Hall of Fame. Robinson was already going to become one of the greatest players in the history of the sport but winning the 1955 World Series only added another accolade to his name.

Retirement

After winning the 1955 World Series against the New York Yankees, who the Dodgers could not beat in the previous four times that they met in the championship, Jackie Robinson probably no longer had anything to prove. He was an MVP, a champion, an All-Star, and was the most well-known black athlete in the entire world at that time. Moreover, Robinson had a lot of impact off the field as he helped inspire his fellow African Americans while also pushing for more black players in the MLB and other major sports as well. He was also one of the main personalities influential in the desegregation of restaurants, hotels, and other public places.

All that said, Jackie Robinson did not have anything else to prove at that point in his career as he was heading towards his tenth season since breaking the color barrier in 1947. At the age of 37, he was already well past his prime years but was still capable enough to run with the younger players in the league. In that regard, it still was not time for Robinson to retire from the game of baseball.

Jackie Robinson made up for what was a poor season during 1955 when the Brooklyn Dodgers won the World Series Championship. After what was his worst season as a baseball star, the six-time All-Star went on to play 117 games during the 1956 season and finished with 61 runs and 98 hits. He had a hitting average of

.275 a year after his .256 batting average a year ago. He also finished with 12 stolen bases that season.

The Brooklyn Dodgers went on to have another dominant season in 1956 as the defending champions went on to secure the National League pennant once more. For the sixth time since acquiring Jackie Robinson in 1947, the Dodgers faced the New York Yankees in the World Series. Nevertheless, Robinson appeared to have played his final game not only for the Dodgers but also in the MLB when he struck out of Game 7 of their World Series loss to the Yankees.

It was during that season when Jackie Robinson changed his mind about wanting to manage a baseball team after his years as a player were done. His health was declining, and he was more interested in his fight for civil rights. Moreover, his relationship with O'Malley had already suffered as well. He never really was too fond of O'Malley ever since the team owner powerplayed his way to kick Branch Rickey off the team. Meanwhile, O'Malley also wanted their once-best player to either focus more on baseball so that he could at least help his team win even if he was no longer the star or to step down from the game for good in a graceful manner. However, Robinson did neither of those.[xiii] This forced the Dodgers to seek drastic measures that the front office believed was good for the franchise's future.

Just after the 1956 season, Walter O'Malley decided to cut his losses with the 37-year-old Jackie Robinson, who he never truly saw eye to eye with ever since Branch Rickey was forced out of the franchise in 1950. As such, the Brooklyn Dodgers made the move to trade Jackie Robinson to the New York Giants in exchange for Dick Littlefield and cash consideration. But Jackie Robinson got the last laugh as the trade never really materialized.

It was revealed that Jackie Robinson had previously agreed to become an executive with the coffee company Chock full o'Nuts. To that effect, he agreed to retire from the game of baseball. Robinson announced his retirement via *Look* magazine, to which he had actually sold his retirement story rights two years before his decision to retire. And because he was effectively no longer with the Brooklyn Dodgers, who wanted to trade him, Jackie Robinson never announced his retirement via the team that signed him back in 1947 when he broke the MLB's color barrier.

Nevertheless, Jackie Robinson had an opportunity to stay with the New York Giants after that retirement announcement on *Look*. The Giants reportedly offered $60,000 to the six-time All-Star to convince him to stay with the MLB. Of course, playing alongside fellow black player and future 24-time All-Star Willie Mays was also quite tempting for Robinson. However, he ended up declining the offer from the Giants when the Dodgers implied that Robinson was merely trying to bargain a larger contract in New York by announcing his retirement.

When Jackie Robinson proved the Dodgers wrong by declining the offer that the Giants made him, his playing career in the MLB was officially over and he was on his way to the second act of his career as a company executive, an activist, and an inspirational figure for many different black Americans. He ended his career with 947 runs, 1518 hits, 197 stolen bases, and a batting average of .311. He was a one-time MVP, a World Series champion in 1955, and a six-time MLB All-Star while playing all of his ten years with the Brooklyn Dodgers.

Chapter 6: Post-Retirement Years

Personal Endeavors and the Fight for Civil Rights

Aside from working as the vice president for Chock full o'Nuts, which made him the first black vice president of an American corporation, Jackie Robinson also spent some time under the spotlight during his post-baseball years as he was someone who just seemed to have the type of personality that allowed him to stay within the media's radar. He served as a board member of Freedom National Bank, which served the purpose of providing loans for minority members who struggled to secure funding from other banking institutions in America. Robinson also spent time writing for a newspaper column and hosting a radio television show, both of which helped him in his crusade against the abuses that his fellow African Americans faced in society.

One of the reasons why Jackie Robinson pursued personal endeavors in business and in the media was that he always believed it was for the purpose of advancing black Americans in the field of commerce and media, where they never really had a lot of opportunities in the past due to how they were left working for farms and in factories as low-wage workers. He was essentially proving that African Americans could also succeed in different endeavors such as business and media.

Being one of the most outspoken persons when it came to black American civil rights, Jackie Robinson eventually got entangled with politics, as his voice was one of those his fellow African Americans relied on when it came to certain political views and issues. And while he later on regretted such a decision, he endorsed Richard Nixon over John F. Kennedy back in 1960 because he felt that Kennedy was not someone who truly made it a point to get to know more about the people of color in America.[xiii] However, he would later praise Kennedy for how he fought well for civil rights.

In 1964, Jackie Robinson became more active in politics when he was one of the six national directors that pushed Nelson Rockefeller to be named the candidate for the Republicans in that year's presidential election. However, it turned out to be an unsuccessful campaign when Barry Goldwater was nominated by the party instead. However, he later worked under Rockefeller when the latter was re-elected as the governor of the state of New York two years later. Jackie Robinson later switched sides to the Democrats in 1968.

In 1965, Jackie Robinson went back to baseball, not as a player but as an analyst for the television network ABC. He became the first black person to serve as a television analyst for baseball. Robinson's voice and his views as a baseball analyst allowed people to realize that people of color were not only supreme athletes who were able to outrun and outperform the competition but were also just as knowledgeable of the game as their white counterparts.

Jackie Robinson, who once dreamed of becoming a team manager earlier in his life, got to live this dream for a while but it was in the sport of football. In the past, there were reports that said that the Brooklyn Dodgers actually offered Robinson the managerial spot of the Montreal Royals after his playing career was done but such an agreement never materialized. However, in 1966, he actually managed the Brooklyn Dodgers of the Continental Football League, but it only lasted for a while. In 1972, he then served as a commentator for the Montreal Expos, a baseball team based in Canada.

Throughout his post-baseball life, Jackie Robinson was outspoken against the MLB's lack of black central office staff and managers. At that point, no team had ever appointed a black man to the managerial post of an MLB team. To that end, he made his final baseball-related public appearance in 1972 when he received a plaque honoring his 25th anniversary as the first black man to play in the MLB. At that moment, he commented that what would make him happier was to see an African American one day managing an MLB team.[xxvii]

Hall of Fame Induction

It was in 1962 that Jackie Robinson became eligible to be nominated into the baseball Hall of Fame as a player. Because the nomination into the Hall of Fame was for his credentials as a baseball player, Robinson urged writers that he should only be named into the Hall of Fame for his credentials on the field rather than for what he meant to the world culturally, politically, and socially.[xxviii] And while Jackie Robinson may have meant more to the world because of his larger-than-baseball contributions as a civil rights activist, it was clear that his on-the-field credentials as a baseball star made him more than worthy to be a Hall of Famer. After all, he was a six-time All-Star, a champion, an MVP, and a player who allowed the Brooklyn Dodgers to become perennial contenders throughout his tenure with the team.

Jackie Robinson, regardless of whether or not his cultural impact was considered, was selected as a first-ballot Hall of Famer. To that effect, Robinson became the first-ever black American player to be inducted into the Cooperstown Baseball Hall of Fame. He was forever enshrined as one of the greatest players to have ever played the game of baseball.

Chapter 7: Family Life and Death

Jackie Robinson was born in Cairo, Georgia, where it was difficult for black people to live because of how they were often exploited by landowners as "slaves" who worked on farms for meager salaries. His mother's side of the family were sharecroppers who spent generations growing crops on lands they did not even own. Meanwhile, Robinson's father was an absentee who always spent time away from the family until he finally left his wife for good for another woman. As such, Jackie Robinson grew up without a true father figure but learned to rely more on his uncles and older brothers for the paternal care he sought.

The Robinsons were gifted athletes, as one of Jackie's older brothers went on to represent the United States in the 1936 Olympic Games in Berlin, Germany and won a silver medal in track and field. His brother's success as an athlete was one of the reasons why Jackie

Robinson was inspired to seek the life of an athlete when he was young.

When Jackie Robinson became a four-sport athlete at UCLA, he met his wife-to-be, Rachel Islum, who was also studying at UCLA back then. She was already familiar with Robinson's athletic exploits at that point in time. The two began a romantic relationship sometime in 1940 when Jackie Robinson was already a senior at UCLA. Jackie and Rachel would later formalize their engagement after Robinson finished Officer Candidate School and received his commission as a second lieutenant in 1943.

The couple got married on February 10, 1946, when Jackie Robinson was already playing baseball for the Negro League. The Robinsons were blessed with their first child, Jackie Robinson Jr., later after getting married in 1946. In 1950, they had their first daughter named Sharon Robinson. And in 1952, their youngest son David Robinson (not the basketball player) was born.

Jackie Robinson Jr. had a troubled early life. He had to seek special education when he was still a boy. Later on, he sought out a more disciplined approach to his life by enrolling in the Army and serving for the United States in the Vietnam War, where he was eventually wounded in 1965. Jackie Jr. ended up with drug problems right after his service to the military but eventually got himself clean and even went on to become a counselor for those who also had drug problems. However, Jackie Robinson Jr. did not outlive his father, as he was killed in a car accident in 1971.[iii] It was his problems with drugs and eventual death that led Jackie Robinson Sr. to become someone who fought hard against drugs and not just for the rights of fellow African Americans.

Jackie Robinson, even though he outlived his eldest son, eventually ended up following Junior the following year. Due to complications from diabetes, Robinson's health rapidly deteriorated to the point that he seemed older than he was. On October 24, 1972, Jack Roosevelt Robinson suffered a heart attack in his home in Connecticut, the immediate cause of his death. He was only 53 years old at that time.

The overwhelming response to his death was a testament to how well-loved and how big of an icon Jackie Robinson was to the eyes of fans and people of color alike. His funeral service attracted more than 2,500 people. Meanwhile, it was estimated that more than 10,000 people lined up for his procession route to morn for Jackie Robinson as he was about to be buried next to his son Jackie Jr. in Cypress Hills Cemetery in Brooklyn.

Jackie Robinson was survived by wife Rachel Robinson, who founded the Jackie Robinson Foundation, daughter Sharon Robinson, who went on to become a midwife and an educator who worked together with the MLB and wrote two books about her father, and son David Robinson, who sought out a career as a coffee grower and also continued his father's fight as a social activist.

Posthumous Recognition

Jackie Robinson, years and decades after his death, continued to make an impact on the entire world and was still getting recognition from international bodies and well-known media publications. In 1999, just when the millennium was about to end, he was named by *TIME* magazine as one of the 100 most influential people of the 20th century together with the likes of Mahatma Gandhi, Albert Einstein, and his namesake Franklin D. Roosevelt.[xxix]

That same year in 1999, Jackie Robinson was also recognized by *Sporting News* as the 44th best player out of the "100 Greatest Players in the History of Baseball." He was even the top vote-getter in the position of second base in the MLB's All-Century

Team. Meanwhile, well-known baseball writer Bill James named Jackie Robinson as the 32nd best player in the history of the game just by basing it on the man's on-the-field abilities instead of factoring in Robinson's contributions to culture, politics, and society. James went on to say that Jackie Robinson deserved such a place because he was always regarded as one of the top players in the entire MLB during his prime years.[xxx]

The MLB also went on to honor Jackie Robinson time and time again. It was in 1987 when they renamed the National and American Leagues Rookie of the Year Award as the Jackie Robinson Award as he was the MLB's inaugural Rookie of the Year Award winner back in 1947 before separate awards were handed out to the National and American League Rookies of the Year. Later in 1997, Jackie Robinson's number 42 jersey was the first number to be retired across all teams in the entire league. Similarly, it was also the first time in all of the four major American sports that a number was retired across the board. On April 15, 2004, Jackie Robinson Day was started, and it required all players in the MLB to wear the number 42 as an exception to the general rule of the number's retirement.

On November 22, 2014, UCLA followed the MLB's example by retiring the number 42 across all of the school's sports in recognition of what Robinson accomplished as an athlete even though he was never able to finish his studies with the university. Jackie Robinson was said to have worn several jersey numbers during his time with UCLA but his number 42 was chosen because it was what was associated with him as a baseball player.

Chapter 8: Impact and Legacy

To say that Jackie Robinson has had an impact is something of an understatement. This extraordinary man was able to make a lasting impact not only on the sport of baseball but on the entire world as well. Baseball was indeed the platform that allowed Jackie Robinson to elevate his name and to forward his personal crusades against racism, but he was always more than just a baseball player in the eyes of a lot of people even to this day. The man was a strong-willed fighter who fought for what was right for his own people and was also one of the many African Americans who made a lasting impact that can still be felt all across America to this day.

Jackie Robinson started his fight against racial oppression when he was still in the military while serving for the Army during World War II. He experienced oppression in the army when his application for the OCS was delayed on account of his race. It took the help of heavyweight boxing legend Joe Louis for his application to the OCS to be accepted. However, his most famous race-related incident in the military occurred when he refused a military bus driver's demand that he should move to the back of the bus. As a result, he was court-martialed but was later on found innocent of the wrongful charges against him. The Jackie Robinson court-martial was a national sensation that made the former second lieutenant a well-known name all over the country even before he made his name as a baseball player.

At that point in time, Jackie Robinson was a fighter who would never back down from authority figures whom he perceived were racist against him and his fellow black Americans. But that was not the kind of person he became when he was eventually taken by Brooklyn Dodgers general manager Branch Rickey in a move that changed the very fabric of professional sports in the United States.

When Branch Rickey handpicked Jackie Robinson to be the man he believed was equipped with the skills, athletic gifts, and personality that would allow him to survive the kind of environment he would face in the MLB, he made it a point to tell the future Hall of Famer that it was best for him to be strong enough to turn the other cheek when facing racial abuse from baseball players and fans alike.

Jackie Robinson, being the fiery and anger-fueled black man that he was at that time, was hesitant to turn the other cheek at first because he thought that doing so was a sign that he was being passive towards racial abuse. However, he later learned from Rickey that he had to prove that he was the bigger man by not retaliating against the insults thrown at him. This was the Jackie Robinson that the world would later come to know and love.

Throughout the earlier portions of his baseball career, Jackie Robinson was the target of many race-related insults from players and fans alike because they did not approve of him breaking the color barrier or with racial integration in the MLB. Fans verbally abused him while opposing players were far too physical with him. But, even in the middle of all that, Jackie Robinson never once retaliated—instead he honored his commitment to Rickey and truly became the better man. His pacifist approach earned him the admiration of the league front office as well as other notable players in the MLB at that time. It also inspired the African Americans of that time to fight the good fight through noble means and not through retaliation.

It cannot be overstated how important it was for Jackie Robinson to show a passive side in the middle of all the racial abuse he was getting in the MLB. At that time, tensions between blacks and whites were so high that there were riots happening between African Americans and authority figures. To that end, it was essential for black people to have a figure to look up to for guidance on what to do whenever they were getting abused and maltreated because of their race. Jackie Robinson was that man.

Black Americans all over the country saw how Jackie Robinson stood up for them, not by fighting or retaliating but by becoming the better and bigger man and by proving that even a person of color can rise up and see success even when the odds are stacked against them. Moreover, Robinson opened opportunities for his fellow blacks to rise up in society by pushing for black integration in the MLB. This led to an influx of African American athletes entering the MLB and making an impact in the league by playing at the highest level possible.

But while Jackie Robinson remained passive on the field as a baseball player, he used his status as one of the greatest players of his generation to push forward his fight for African American civil rights. He was often critical of MLB teams who were not yet open to signing black players into their roster. Robinson was also quite outspoken when it came to political and social issues regarding racism and how his fellow black people were getting mistreated. To this end, a lot of restaurants and hotels began abolishing their segregation policies and allowed black people the equal opportunity to enjoy their services.

Jackie Robinson ended his baseball career after a fruitful and stellar ten-year run with the Brooklyn Dodgers. However, his fight did not end as he sought out to push his support for civil rights in other avenues. His success as a businessman was a testament to how black people were just as skilled in such endeavors as white people. Of course, Robinson was also politically active and was openly endorsing and supporting politicians and personalities he believed were progressive in the way they approached the Civil Rights Movement and the fight of African Americans for equal rights in the United States.

Jackie Robinson essentially helped start a movement that allowed black people to use whatever platform they had to voice their concerns and to fight for equal opportunities and treatment rather than to take their fight to the streets. There have now been countless black personalities who have used their own individual success to push for the rights of their people while making the fight as passive and as peaceful as possible, much in the same way that Jackie Robinson fought for civil rights. Many popular black athletes later followed Robinson's example, as notable names in many different sports in American surfaced and used their status to inspire a new generation of African Americans to rise above the maltreatment and use whatever platform they had to elevate themselves and fight for the rights of their fellow blacks.

While Jackie Robinson did indeed have a stellar career as a baseball player after making six trips to the All-Star Game, winning an MVP, and securing a World Series Championship, he still is remembered best for breaking the color barrier. Jackie Robinson made it possible for athletes of any color or race to make it big in America and to use their gifts and skills to make a difference in society without using violence and antagonistic means as a way of making things better.

As such, there is no denying that, while Jackie Robinson was an athlete, his biggest contributions were seen in the areas outside of the baseball field. He permeated society like no other player before him ever had with his inspiring rise to stardom and with his fight for equal rights and opportunities for his fellow African Americans. There may never again be someone as impactful as Jackie Robinson was. That is why he will always be regarded as one of the greatest individuals the world has ever seen.

Final Word/About the Author

I was born and raised in Norwalk, Connecticut. Growing up, I could often be found spending many nights watching baseball, basketball, soccer, and football matches with my father in the family living room. I love sports and everything that sports can embody. I believe that sports are one of most genuine forms of competition, heart, and determination. I write my works to learn more about influential athletes in the hopes that from my writing, you the reader can walk away inspired to put in an equal if not greater amount of hard work and perseverance to pursue your goals. If you enjoyed *Jackie Robinson: The Inspiring Story of One of Baseball's Greatest Legends,* please leave a review! Also, you can read more of my works on *Aaron Judge, Serena Williams, Rafael Nadal, Roger Federer, Novak Djokovic, Richard Sherman, Andrew Luck, Rob Gronkowski, Brett Favre, Calvin Johnson, Drew Brees, J.J. Watt, Colin Kaepernick, Aaron Rodgers, Peyton Manning, Tom Brady, Russell*

Wilson, Gregg Popovich, Pat Riley, John Wooden, Steve Kerr, Brad Stevens, Red Auerbach, Doc Rivers, Erik Spoelstra, Michael Jordan, LeBron James, Kyrie Irving, Klay Thompson, Stephen Curry, Kevin Durant, Russell Westbrook, Anthony Davis, Chris Paul, Blake Griffin, Kobe Bryant, Joakim Noah, Scottie Pippen, Carmelo Anthony, Kevin Love, Grant Hill, Tracy McGrady, Vince Carter, Patrick Ewing, Karl Malone, Tony Parker, Allen Iverson, Hakeem Olajuwon, Reggie Miller, Michael Carter-Williams, John Wall, James Harden, Tim Duncan, Steve Nash, Draymond Green, Kawhi Leonard, Dwyane Wade, Ray Allen, Pau Gasol, Dirk Nowitzki, Jimmy Butler, Paul Pierce, Manu Ginobili, Pete Maravich, Larry Bird, Kyle Lowry, Jason Kidd, David Robinson, LaMarcus Aldridge, Derrick Rose, Paul George, Kevin Garnett, Chris Paul, Marc Gasol, Yao Ming, Al Horford, Amar'e Stoudemire, DeMar DeRozan, Isaiah Thomas, Kemba Walker, Chris Bosh, Andre Drummond, JJ Redick, DeMarcus Cousins, Wilt Chamberlain, Bradley Beal,

112

Rudy Gobert, Aaron Gordon, Kristaps Porzingis, Nikola Vucevic, Andre Iguodala, Devin Booker, John Stockton, Jeremy Lin, Chris Paul, Pascal Siakam, Jayson Tatum, Gordon Hayward, Nikola Jokic, Bill Russell, Victor Oladipo, Luka Doncic, Ben Simmons, Shaquille O'Neal, Joel Embiid, Donovan Mitchell, Damian Lillard and Giannis Antetokounmpo in the Kindle Store. If you love baseball, check out my website at claytongeoffreys.com to join my exclusive list where I let you know about my latest books and give you lots of goodies.

Like what you read? Please leave a review!

I write because I love sharing the stories of influential athletes like Jackie Robinson with fantastic readers like you. My readers inspire me to write more so please do not hesitate to let me know what you thought by leaving a review! If you love books on life, baseball, or productivity, check out my website at claytongeoffreys.com to join my exclusive list where I let you know about my latest books. Aside from being the first to hear about my latest releases, you can also download a free copy of *33 Life Lessons: Success Principles, Career Advice & Habits of Successful People*. See you there!

Clayton

References

[i] "Breaking the Color Line: 1940 to 1946". *Library of Congress*. Web.

[ii] Rampersad, Arnold. "In Pharaoh's Land: Cairo, Georgia 1919-1920". *Jackie Robinson: A Biography*. Web.

[iii] Robinson, Rachel; with Daniels, Lee. "Jackie Robinson: An Intimate Portrait." New York: Harry N. Abrams. 1996.

[iv] Rampersad, Arnold. "Jackie Robinson: A Biography". New York: Alfred A. Knopf. 1997

[v] Stone, Bob. "Sports: Jackie Robinson". *Yank, the Army Weekly*. 23 November 1945. Web

[vi] Greenwald, Dave. "Alumnus Jackie Robinson honored by Congress". *UCLA Athletics*. 1 February 2005. Web.

[vii] Tygiel, Jules. "The Court-Martial of Jackie Robinson". *American Heritage*. 19 November 2008. Web.

[viii] O'Connell, Jack. "Robinson's many peers follow his lead". *MLB.com*. 13 April 2007. Web.

[ix] Paige, Satchel; David Lipman. "Maybe I'll pitch forever: a great baseball player tells the hilarious story behind the legend". 1993. *U of Nebraska Press*. pp. xi, xii.

[x] Lamb, Chris. "Opinion: The redemption of Clay Hopper". *Montreal Gazette*. 7 April 2013. Web.

[xi] "Royals' Game Off at Jacksonville". *New York Times*. 23 March 1946. Web.

[xii] "US to honor Robinson's Montreal home". *FOXSports.com*. Associated Press. February 27, 2011. Web.

[xiii] Swaine, Rick. "SABR Biography of Jackie Robinson". *Society for American Baseball Research*. Web.

[xiv] Schwartz, Larry. "Jackie changed face of sports". *ESPN*. 10 April 2010. Web.

[xv] "Jackie Robinson breaks major league color barrier". *History Channel*. Web.

[xvi] Wormser, Richard. "Jackie Robinson integrates Baseball". *Public Broadcasting Service*. 2002.

[xvii] Newman, Mark. "1947: A time for change". *MLB.com*. 13 April 2007. Web.

[xviii] Mathews, Jack. "'Greenberg' A Home Run". *New York Daily News*. 12 January 2000. Web.

[xix] Huhn, Rick. "Full circle". The Sizzler: George Sisler, Baseball's Forgotten Great. *Columbia: University of Missouri Press*. 2004.

[xx] ""Did You See Jackie Robinson Hit That Ball?"". *Library of Congress*. Web.

[xxi] Johnson, Chuck. "An All-Star Game for all". *USA Today*. 13 July 1999. Web.

[xxii] Tygiel, Jules (1983). *Baseball's Great Experiment: Jackie Robinson and His Legacy*. New York: Oxford University Press.

[xxiii] Robinson, Jackie (1972). "Breaking the Color Barrier". *I Never Had It Made*. New York: G.P. Putnam's Sons

[xxiv] Duberman, Martin (1989). Paul Robeson. New York: Knopf.

[xxv] Robinson, Jackie. Letter to Branch Rickey. *Library of Congress*. 1950. Web.

[xxvi] Bloom, Barry. "Robinson made impact on field, too". *MLB.com*. 13 April 2007. Web.

[xxvii] Helyar, John. "Robinson would have mixed view of today's game". *ESPN*. 9 April 2007. Web.

[xxviii] "Robinson honored with new Hall of Fame plaque". *ESPN*. June 25, 2008. Web.

[xxix] "Time 100: Jackie Robinson". *Time*. June 14, 1999.

[xxx] James, Bill (2003). "The Players". The New Bill James Historical Baseball Abstract. New York: Free Press.

Made in the USA
Columbia, SC
24 April 2022

59382775R00067